Y0-CAZ-415

Authority
of the
Believer

Study Guide

KENNETH COPELAND

Authority of the Believer

Study Guide

KENNETH COPELAND

KENNETH COPELAND
PUBLICATIONS

Unless otherwise noted, all scripture is from the *King James Version* of the Bible.

Authority of the Believer Study Guide

ISBN-10   1-57562-708-6   30-0728
ISBN-13   978-1-57562-708-3

23 22 21 20 19 18   11 10 9 8 7

© 1983 International Church of the Word of Faith Inc. now known as Eagle Mountain International Church Inc. aka Kenneth Copeland Ministries

Kenneth Copeland Publications
Fort Worth, TX 76192-0001

For more information about Kenneth Copeland Ministries, visit kcm.org or call 1-800-600-7395 (U.S. only) or +1-817-852-6000.

Printed in the United States of America. All rights reserved under International Copyright Law. No part of this book may be reproduced or transmitted in any form or by any means, electronic or mechanical, including photocopying, recording, or by any information storage and retrieval system, without the written permission of the publisher.

1

"And God said, Let us make man in our image, after our likeness: and let them have dominion over the fish of the sea, and over the fowl of the air, and over the cattle, and over all the earth, and over every creeping thing that creepeth upon the earth."

Genesis 1:26

In the image of God…Man was

created to have authority.

CD ONE
Authority of the Believer I

Jesus Went to the Cross to Buy Back the Authority Adam Lost...Believers Have Authority Through Their Union With Jesus

God Uses Words of Faith and Authority to Create…So Can You!

FOCUS: "Through faith we understand that the worlds were framed by the word of God, so that things which are seen were not made of things which do appear" (Hebrews 11:3).

God operates by faith. He does nothing apart from faith. Hebrews 11:6 says, "But without faith it is impossible to please him: for he that cometh to God must believe that he is, and that he is a rewarder of them that diligently seek him."

When God saw everything He had made, He beheld that it was very good (Genesis 1:31). Adam was created in the image and likeness of God and God is a faith being. He used words of authority to create man.

Hebrews 11:1 says that "faith is the substance of things hoped for, the evidence of things not seen." The worlds were framed by the words God spoke. He used an unseen substance to speak into existence things we see. "Through faith we understand that the worlds were framed by the word of God" so that things which are seen were not made out of something that can be seen (Hebrews 11:3). Faith is the original force that cannot be seen. It is the parent force to everything in this planet.

God communicated His faith and released it in words. He creates with His Word. Words paint pictures. When God releases His faith, the words He speaks come to pass. He knows how to use words to their fullest extent and power. In Genesis 1:3, God said, "Let there be light," and there was. He took words, filled with power, and spoke a universe into existence.

The Holy Spirit uses the substance of faith in the words to cause the desired result to come into physical manifestation.

When the believer takes the Word of God and meditates upon it, the Holy Spirit creates in him the inner image of the Word of God. God sent Jesus so that, as new creations, we could live the abundant life. We have been predestined to be conformed to the image of Jesus (Romans 8:29). It is through the revelation of the Word that we will see ourselves this way.

> *Authority is transferred and carried out by words.*

This earth and everything in it came into being by words. Authority is transferred and carried out by words. Words are used to communicate.

God's Word is His bond with man. His covenant cannot be annulled or canceled.

God gave man authority in the natural world as well as the spiritual world. Man is a spirit, he has a soul made up of his mind, will and emotions, and he lives in a body. He was created in God's image—a triune being. He has authority in the earth because he has a physical body made from the earth—he is a spirit living in a body. He has an intellectual capacity that is above the animals. He has dominion in three worlds—spirit, soul and physical.

Adam lost sight of the authority God had given him and walked away from it when he bowed his knee to Satan. Jesus went to the cross to buy back, with His own life, the dominion and authority that God originally gave Adam.

*We can take advantage of
the authority that has been given to
us through our union with Jesus.*

Now Begin Enjoying It

Hebrews 1:3 says He is upholding all things by the Word of His power. If you want to be upheld, get on the Word. Make up your mind to speak only what God has said.

Make this a vital part of your life through meditation in God's Word. It will not only reveal the Word to you, but the revelation of this will change everything around you because this is the way God operates. When you learn to operate the way He does, you will experience the victory and success He provided for you.

CD 1 Outlined

I. Everything God does is by faith
  A. Adam was created in God's image
  B. God is a faith being

II. God creates with His Word
  A. He releases faith with words
    1. Faith is substance
    2. Words create
  B. The Holy Spirit causes words to manifest

III. Everything is based on words
  A. Authority is transferred by words
  B. Words communicate

IV. Man was given authority under God
  A. He had dominion in three worlds
    1. Spiritual realm
    2. Soul—mental superiority
    3. Body—earthly authority
  B. Adam lost sight of and walked away from the authority God had given him
  C. Jesus bought back man's authority

Study Questions

(1) How does God operate? _____

_____

_____

_____

(2) Explain how words of faith operate. _____

_____

_____

_____

(3) What do words have to do with authority? _____

_____

_____

_____

(4) Why is it possible for man to have authority in three realms?

_____

_____

_____

(5) How can you as a born-again believer apply this authority to your life?

_____

_____

_____

Study Notes

*"Through faith we understand that the
worlds were framed by the word of God...."*
Hebrews 11:3

2

"For verily I say unto you, That whosoever shall say unto this mountain, Be thou removed, and be thou cast into the sea; and shall not doubt in his heart, but shall believe that those things which he saith shall come to pass; he shall have whatsoever he saith."

Mark 11:23

The words you speak bring what you are

believing for into the here and now.

CD TWO
Authority of the Believer II

The Believer Has the Creative Power of God Inside Him— God's Creative Power Is Released in Words

Learn to Use Your Authority...
In the Here and Now!

FOCUS: "And Jesus came and spake unto them, saying, All power is given unto me in heaven and in earth. Go ye therefore..." (Matthew 28:18-19).

God has invested authority in the Body of Christ. It is not for use in heaven. The authority of the Lord Jesus Christ has been invested in the Body of Christ to operate here in the earth.

Man has been given the ability to choose and speak words at his own will. Authority is communicated by words. God created everything that can be seen with words. Words paint pictures and as faith is activated in those words, they come to pass.

Something starts out as an image on the inside and words describe that picture. Adequate words can transfer the image from the inside of one person to another. Everything that can be seen was originally an image before it was a reality. This universe was an image on the inside of God before it became a reality.

> *Our confession is one of authority.*

The words you speak will bring the thing you are believing for into the here and now. Jesus said to speak to the mountains and tell them to be removed. God's creative power is released in words.

A born-again child of God has the creative power of God inside him. The fruit of the spirit is inside him. The same creative faith God used when He spoke this universe into existence is inside the believer.

When God created man, He spoke words and brought him into existence the same way He spoke words and brought this planet into existence.

Whenever God speaks, the Holy Spirit takes the substance of faith and brings those words into existence. When you speak, the Spirit of God will move because that same authority is in you.

What He did in you when you were born again is greater than what Satan did in Adam. Death has been swallowed up in life.

So what should our confession be? Our confession is one of authority, of humility. The born-again believer has been made a new creation in Christ Jesus. He is not self-righteous but the righteousness of God in Christ.

Man was brought into existence equipped with the same authority that God used in creating him. He gave a covenant to man, delegating that authority to him.

Adam committed high treason, giving his authority to Satan, as an act of his will. He was the first man ever to be born again from life to death. Satan's nature was lodged in his spirit.

> *God gave a covenant to man, delegating authority to him.*

In Luke 4:6-7 Jesus was tempted by Satan. Satan said that he would give Jesus all power or authority if He would worship him. Satan had it to give or he would not have offered it to Jesus.

Jesus knew He had to go to the cross to legally obtain man's redemption and give him back his authority. He responded with the Word instead of acting on what Satan said. Jesus passed the test that Adam failed.

When we see how far-reaching Adam's authority was,

we see the lengths Jesus went to in order to redeem mankind. Man was the key figure in the Fall, so man had to be the key figure in redemption. There had to be a man like that first one, Adam. The treason Adam committed reached from heaven to the lowest part of the earth. God had given man such authority that the Fall affected three worlds of existence: heaven, earth and under the earth. This treason perverted everything.

Jesus took back the keys...for you!

Jesus went to hell and paid the price for man's sins. Jesus did not sin; He became sin. He bore man's sin—was man's substitute. He died for the sins of the world.

Then the Spirit of God went into the bowels of hell, into Satan's domain, and unleashed the creative power of God to make Jesus alive again.

Jesus took back the authority that Adam had lost and carried His blood into the holy of holies. He ratified a new covenant, purged man's sins and cleansed the heavenly utensils of worship with His own blood. Jesus went to great lengths to redeem man and restore his authority.

Now Begin Enjoying It

Jesus has made the born-again believer His representative in the earth.

God's creative power is inside you. So choose words of faith and speak your authority. It's yours for the taking!

$\mathcal{CD}$ 2 *Outlined*

I. Man can choose the words he speaks
    A. Words paint pictures
    B. Words communicate
    C. Words become manifestations
    D. Creative power is released in words

II. God delegated authority to man

III. Adam committed high treason and took on
    Satan's nature

IV. Jesus acted on God's Word
    A. He yielded to God
    B. He passed the test Adam failed
    C. He ratified a new covenant

V. Jesus became sin
    A. He did not commit sin
    B. He was the substitute

VI. The authority that raised Jesus from the dead raised
    you from the dead

VII. The believer is Jesus' representative on earth

Study Questions

(1) Explain what has to take place before words become reality. _____

_____

_____

_____

_____

(2) Why can the believer boldly confess who he is? _____

_____

_____

_____

_____

(3) What happened when Adam committed high treason? _____

_____

_____

_____

_____

(4) Explain why Jesus had to go to the lengths He went to in order to redeem man. _____

_____

_____

_____

(5) What happens on the inside of a man who accepts Jesus? _____

_____

_____

_____

_____

Study Notes

"But what saith it? The word is nigh thee, even in thy mouth, and in thy heart: that is, the word of faith, which we preach."
Romans 10:8

3

"And ye are complete in him [Christ], which is the head of all principality and power.... And having spoiled principalities and powers, he made a show of them openly, triumphing over them in it."

Colossians 2:10, 15

A born-again man defeated hell.

You've been reborn with the same power.

CD THREE
Authority of the Believer III

Jesus Became Like Us So We Could Become Like Him

We are joint heirs, seated with Jesus in a heavenly place of authority. (Romans 8:17; Ephesians 2:6)

You're Not What You Used to Be—You Have Authority in Christ!

FOCUS: "Therefore if any man be in Christ, he is a new creature: old things are passed away; behold, all things are become new" (2 Corinthians 5:17).

The authority given to the believer is part of the redemptive work that Jesus did in man's behalf. He became like man so man could become like Him.

The born-again believer has been made a new creation. He is created in the image and likeness of God. He has the same capacity for faith that Jesus has. He has the same capacity to love that Jesus has.

Romans 5:5 says that the love of God has been shed abroad in our hearts by the Holy Ghost. If there were no capacity for it, He could not have put it there. God made man in His image so that He could have fellowship with someone in His own class.

> *Jesus regained authority for man.*

What you were before salvation has nothing to do with who you are now. The old man is dead and gone. Old things have passed away.

The reason God sent Jesus into the earth was to destroy the work of Satan and give back to man the authority he lost through Adam's transgression. Jesus had to go through the same thing Adam went through for it to be legal. Jesus did not commit sin. He was not a sinner, yet He died the death of a sinner. He made Himself obedient to death.

Jesus took on Himself the nature of sin and gave us His righteousness. We were made righteous. Faith, through grace, caused God to make us righteous. It was not through works.

See yourself alive in Him. See Jesus paying the price for your redemption at Calvary. If He did not actually die, you would not have access to redemption.

What Jesus did was for mankind, not for Himself. He did not gain authority over Satan for Himself. He already had authority over the devil. He came to obtain it for you. He gained authority over Satan so the Body of Christ could wear the full armor of God and have the authority to use His Name. He bought it with His own blood.

Jesus put Himself into the hands of Satan. He was ushered into hell to suffer but He was taken there illegally. All mankind and all authority over mankind belonged to Satan, who was called the god of this world. Satan took Jesus in there, thinking he had God right where he wanted Him. For three days and nights in the depths of hell, Jesus was tormented.

In the pit of hell, God spoke words of authority. Hebrews 1 says that God brought the first begotten into the world. He was justified and made alive in the spirit. To *justify* is to "make righteous," to "put in right-standing with the Father." You were justified with Him and have been made the righteousness of God in Christ Jesus. He was raised from the dead. You were raised from the dead. He was the first man ever to be born again from death to life. The new birth occurred in the depths of hell. Jesus defeated Satan, triumphed over him in the cross and regained the authority for man.

> *You are a joint heir with the King of kings.*

> *You have been made alive in Christ. The same power that put Jesus at the right hand of God put you at His right hand. You are a joint heir with the King of kings. You are walking in covenant with Almighty God through Jesus Christ.*

You are His workmanship created in Christ Jesus (Ephesians 2:10). It was the creative power of God that worked in you when you accepted Jesus as Lord. You're not what you used to be. You're a new creature—with authority—*in Christ.*

Now Begin Enjoying It

Take your place as a joint heir and begin to walk in your covenant rights. Learn to use your authority in Christ Jesus to stand against Satan and he will flee!

CD 3 Outlined

I. The believer is a new creation in Christ with the same capacity to love as Jesus

II. Jesus took man's sin and gave him His righteousness

III. Jesus defeated Satan for mankind
   A. Jesus already had authority
   B. Jesus took away Satan's authority and gave it back to man

IV. The believer walks in covenant with Jesus

Study Questions

(1) Why did God make man in His image? _____
_____
_____
_____

(2) Why is it important to see that Jesus paid the price for your redemption at Calvary? _____
_____
_____
_____

(3) What does justify *mean? How are you justified?* _____
_____
_____
_____
_____

(4) Where did the new birth of Jesus take place? What happened there? _____
_____
_____
_____
_____

(5) Explain the significance of walking in covenant with God through the new birth. _____
_____
_____
_____

Study Notes

*"By the obedience of one [Jesus]
shall many be made righteous."*
Romans 5:19

4

"*For whom he did foreknow, he also did predestinate to be conformed to the image of his Son....*"

Romans 8:29

God sees you in Christ, in His image.

How do you see yourself?

CD FOUR
Authority of the Believer IV

God Sees You Through
the Blood of the
Covenant...Inside,
You Are the Express
Image of Jesus

Seeing You Should Be the
Same as Seeing Jesus

FOCUS: "I am crucified with Christ: nevertheless I live; yet not I, but Christ liveth in me..." (Galatians 2:20).

When God spoke, things were brought into existence. He created man in His image and likeness. Adam was made by God to have all of His attributes, all of His authority, all of His faith and all of His ability.

It is commonly understood that God has authority and that Jesus has authority. But traditional thinking has set the authority of Jesus on a high plateau and the

> *Jesus gave the Body of Christ the same authority He has.*

authority of the believer on a much lower plateau. In the light of God's Word, we see that Jesus gave the Body of Christ the same authority He has.

Jesus came to the earth and met man on his level. He came to pay Adam's price for high treason. He came to reconcile man back to God. He defeated Satan in hell, took from him the authority that Adam had given him, and was raised to the right hand of God.

Jesus did not sin; He took man's sin and died the death of a sinner. But He didn't stay that way. He was raised from the dead. Upon raising Jesus from the dead, God called Him God and said His throne is forever (Hebrews 1:8). He will never die again. The universe was put into the hands of a born-again, resurrected, glorified man.

Jesus said, "All power is given unto me in heaven and in earth" (Matthew 28:18). He conferred this same authority on the believer and gave him the power of attorney to use His Name.

Hebrews 1 is a picture of Jesus after He was raised from the dead. Verse 3 says, "Who being the brightness of his glory, and the express image of his person...." Seeing Jesus is seeing God. Jesus is the express, absolute image of God. Everything in God is expressed again in Jesus, every likeness and every detail.

Romans 8:29 says, "For whom he did foreknow, he also did predestinate to be conformed to the image of his Son...." Verse 32 says that God delivered Jesus up for us all. He was raised in the image of God, and all who accept Him as Lord are raised up in the same expressed image.

As born-again believers, we have authority; we are in His image. Meditation upon this will give us an inner image so we can see ourselves as God sees us. We will be able to go to the throne of grace boldly (Hebrews 4:16). God is looking at us through the blood covenant.

He looks at the inside of a man—
upon the heart. He sees us in
Christ, in His image.

Now Begin Enjoying It

Now begin seeing yourself as God sees you—in Christ, having authority—and start walking in it!

CD 4 Outlined

I. Jesus bought back man's authority
   A. He paid the price for Adam's treason
   B. He defeated Satan in hell
   C. He was raised to the right hand of God

II. Jesus conferred His authority on the believer

III. God expressed His image in Jesus
   A. The believer is conformed to His image
   B. Believers have authority as He has authority
   C. God sees the believer in His image

IV. Meditation on the Word builds an inner image

Study Questions

(1) Why did Jesus meet man on his level? _____

_____

_____

_____

_____

(2) How do we have the same authority Jesus had? _____

_____

_____

_____

_____

*(3) Explain the attributes of God and why it is important that we be
developed in them as born-again believers.* _____

_____

_____

_____

_____

(4) Explain the passage "Thy throne, O God, is forever." _____

_____

_____

_____

_____

(5) Why do you have kingly and priestly rights? _____

_____

_____

_____

Study Notes

"For whom he did foreknow, he also did predestinate to be conformed to the image of his Son, that he might be the firstborn among many brethren."

Romans 8:29

5

"[God] hath raised us up together, and made us sit together in heavenly places in Christ Jesus."

Ephesians 2:6

In Christ you have been raised

to the same high place of authority

where Jesus sits.

CD FIVE
Authority of the Believer V

All Things Are Under Jesus' Feet—As Part of the Body of Christ, All Things Are Under Your Feet

You Are Seated With Christ...

FOCUS: "Far above all principality, and power, and might, and dominion, and every name that is named, not only in this world, but also in that which is to come: and hath put all things under his feet, and gave him to be the head over all things to the church, which is his body, the fulness of him that filleth all in all" (Ephesians 1:21-23).

When Jesus Christ is accepted as Lord, the life of God is imparted to the spirit of a man. He becomes a new creature. His body and mind are not born again, but his spirit man is.

Man is a spirit, he has a soul, and he lives in a body. The spirit can live without a body, but the body cannot live without the spirit. The spirit man is the life.

It is the spirit man that experiences the new birth and becomes the express image of Christ. You have been predestined in the mind of God, before He ever put the plan of redemption into motion, to be made in the very image of Jesus. The same spiritual qualities and the same authority inside Him is inside you.

Ephesians 1:3 says, "Blessed be the God and Father of our Lord Jesus Christ, who hath blessed us with all spiritual blessings in heavenly places in Christ." *Blessing* means "to say something good about." A blessing of God is to walk in the light of something He has already said. You have already been blessed with all spiritual blessings because you are seated with Him in heavenly places (Ephesians 2:6).

First John 4:17 says, "...As he is, so are we in this world." You are His image expressed to this world.

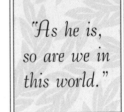

"*As he is, so are we in this world.*"

Jesus is not sick, in poverty, in fear or under pressure. As He is, so are you. His authority, His Name, His position with God have already been given to you. What the Word says about you is what you are. Prayer becomes uncomplicated when you know who you are because you see yourself as God sees you.

Study the Word and find out what God has already said about you. You are seated with Christ far above all principalities, power, might, dominion and every name that is named. All things have been put under His feet. Every name in this earth has been put under the feet of the Body of Christ. Jesus is the Head and the Church is His Body. They are joined together. A revelation of this will show you what kind of authority you have as a believer.

Colossians 2:9-10 says, "For in him dwelleth all the fulness of the Godhead bodily. And ye are complete in him, which is the head of all principality and power." The fullness of the Godhead is residing in the believer. Whoever is joined to the Lord is one spirit with Him.

You represent Jesus! You can walk in authority in His Name because you are His representative. When this becomes a reality to you, sin will lose its grip on you. Renewing your mind to these facts in the Word of God will

*transform and change the entire
attitude of your mind. You will see
yourself in Christ, part of His Body,
with everything under your feet.
Instead of ignoring problems, you
will conquer them with the authority
He has given you. The battle is the
Lord's and the victory is yours.*

Now Begin Enjoying It

Stand in His victory, using the Word, fighting the good fight of
faith. When you speak the Word in faith, it is the same power as if
Almighty God Himself said it, and circumstances will have to come
in line.

CD 5 Outlined

I. The spirit of a man is born again when Jesus is accepted as Lord
   A. God's nature is expressed in the spirit
   B. His abilities become the believer's abilities

II. The believer expresses God's image to the world
   A. 1 John 4:17
   B. Romans 8:29

III. What the Word says about you is what you are
   A. Seated with Him above everything
   B. He is the Head, you are the body
      1. Colossians 2:9-10
      2. 1 Corinthians 6:17

IV. The Word of God from the believer's mouth carries God's authority

Study Questions

(1) Explain why the body cannot live without the spirit. _____

_____

_____

_____

_____

(2) What happens to the spirit of a man who accepts Jesus as Lord?

_____

_____

_____

_____

(3) What does blessing *mean? Why has the believer already been blessed?*

_____

_____

_____

_____

(4) How can you apply 1 John 4:17 to you personally? _____

_____

_____

_____

_____

(5) What does it mean to be in the Body of Christ? _____

_____

_____

_____

_____

Study Notes

"That the Gentiles should be fellowheirs, and of the same body,
and partakers of his promise in Christ by the gospel."
Ephesians 3:6

6

"Wherefore God also hath highly exalted him, and given him a name which is above every name: that at the name of Jesus every knee should bow, of things in heaven, and things in earth, and things under the earth."

Philippians 2:9-10

The power behind the Name of Jesus

is the power of Almighty God.

CD SIX
Authority of the Believer VI

All the Authority of God's Word Is Invested in the Name of Jesus

"*H*is name is called The Word of God." (Revelation 19:13)

Believers Have the Right to Use the Name of Jesus

FOCUS: "...Whatsoever ye shall ask the Father *in my name,* he will give it you" (John 16:23).

In Acts 3:1-8, Peter and John ministered to a lame man at the Beautiful gate. Peter used the Name of Jesus to set the man free. Verse 10 says the people were "filled with wonder and amazement at that which had happened unto him." Peter immediately answered them saying:

> "Ye men of Israel, why marvel ye at this? or why look ye so earnestly on us, as though by our own power or holiness we had made this man to walk.... [Jesus'] name through faith in his name hath made this man strong, whom ye see and know: yea, the faith which is by him hath given him this perfect soundness in the presence of you all" (verses 12, 16).

The healing did not take place because they were apostles or had special holiness from God. These men were simply using the power and authority of the Name of Jesus. They spoke His Name in faith and expected that Name to bring results.

The Name of Jesus is just as powerful today as it was when Peter spoke it. Jesus said, "... Whatsoever ye shall ask the Father in my name, he will give

> *The Name of Jesus is still powerful today.*

it you" (John 16:23). The believer has the right to use the Name of Jesus in every circumstance and situation of life.

The greatness of His Name is threefold. The first one is found in Hebrews 1:4: "As he hath by inheritance obtained a more excellent name...." To understand how much power is backing a name, it has to be measured by the resources of the person from whom it is inherited. If a name is good, it carries with it power and authority. To measure the power behind the Name of Jesus would be to measure the power of Almighty God.

> *Jesus' Name can do anything He can do.*

Find out how much power is behind Him and you will discover how much power is in His Name. His Name can do anything He can do. He is totally unlimited.

The second way Jesus received the greatness of His Name was that God conferred it upon Him. Jesus was given a Name that is above every name, and all things were placed under His feet (Ephesians 1:21-22). After He was raised from the dead, God turned to Him and called Him God. Hebrews 1:8 says, "But unto the Son he saith, Thy throne, O God, is for ever and ever...." There has been conferred upon Jesus a Name with such authority that even at the sound of that Name, every knee shall bow (Philippians 2:9-10).

The third area in which Jesus received the greatness of His Name was by conquest. He achieved it through triumph over Satan. Colossians 2:15 says, "And having spoiled principalities and powers, he made a show of them openly, triumphing over them in it." He went into the bowels of hell itself and defeated Satan. He paid the price for Adam's high treason, leaving Satan stripped of all his power and authority. Jesus took the rights to that Name by conquest.

Jesus gave the Church authority to use His Name to bring salvation and deliverance to all the world. This Name is a weapon to use to enforce Satan's defeat.

Now Begin Enjoying It

Meditate on the power the Name of Jesus carries until it becomes real to you. You can use it effectively when you have a revelation of its power. You will have results. Revelation 19:13 says that His Name is called The Word of God. All of the authority of God's Word is in that Name and it is yours to use as a new creation in Him!

CD 6 Outlined

I. Peter uses the Name of Jesus
   A. Acts 3:1-16, 4:8-10
   B. His Name is not for apostles only

II. The believer needs the Name and has the right to use it

III. The greatness of the Name is threefold
   A. Hebrews 1:1-5—He inherited His Name from God
   B. Philippians 2:9-10—His Name was conferred upon Him by the Father
      1. Ephesians 1:21-22
      2. Hebrews 1:8
   C. Colossians 2:15—He achieved the authority of His Name by conquest
      1. Hebrews 2:14—His conquest over Satan in hell
      2. Luke 11:21-22—He took Satan's armor

Study Questions

(1) Was the lame man healed because Peter was an apostle? _____

_____

_____

_____

_____

(2) Why is the power Jesus inherited so great? _____

_____

_____

_____

_____

(3) Explain how Jesus' Name was conferred upon Him. _____

_____

_____

_____

_____

(4) What did Jesus have to do in order to conquer Satan? _____

_____

_____

_____

_____

(5) How does the Name of Jesus apply to you personally? _____

_____

_____

_____

_____

Study Notes

"*Being made so much better than the angels, as he hath by inheritance obtained a more excellent name....*"

Hebrews 1:4

Prayer for Salvation and Baptism in the Holy Spirit

Heavenly Father, I come to You in the Name of Jesus. Your Word says, "Whosoever shall call on the name of the Lord shall be saved" (Acts 2:21). I am calling on You. I pray and ask Jesus to come into my heart and be Lord over my life according to Romans 10:9-10: "If thou shalt confess with thy mouth the Lord Jesus, and shalt believe in thine heart that God hath raised him from the dead, thou shalt be saved. For with the heart man believeth unto righteousness; and with the mouth confession is made unto salvation." I do that now. I confess that Jesus is Lord, and I believe in my heart that God raised Him from the dead. I repent of sin. I renounce it. I renounce the devil and everything he stands for. Jesus is my Lord.

I am now reborn! I am a Christian—a child of Almighty God! I am saved! You also said in Your Word, "If ye then, being evil, know how to give good gifts unto your children: HOW MUCH MORE shall your heavenly Father give the Holy Spirit to them that ask him?" (Luke 11:13). I'm also asking You to fill me with the Holy Spirit. Holy Spirit, rise up within me as I praise God. I fully expect to speak with other tongues as You give me the utterance (Acts 2:4). In Jesus' Name. Amen!

Begin to praise God for filling you with the Holy Spirit. Speak those words and syllables you receive—not in your own language, but the language given to you by the Holy Spirit. You have to use your own voice. God will not force you to speak. Don't be concerned with how it sounds. It is a heavenly language!

Continue with the blessing God has given you and pray in the spirit every day.

You are a born-again, Spirit-filled believer. You'll never be the same!

Find a good church that boldly preaches God's Word and obeys it. Become part of a church family who will love and care for you as you love and care for them.

We need to be connected to each other. It increases our strength in God. It's God's plan for us.

Make it a habit to watch the Believer's Voice of Victory Network and become a doer of the Word, who is blessed in his doing (James 1:22-25).

About the Author

Kenneth Copeland is co-founder and president of Kenneth Copeland Ministries in Fort Worth, Texas, and best-selling author of books that include *Honor—Walking in Honesty, Truth and Integrity,* and *THE BLESSING of The LORD Makes Rich and He Adds No Sorrow With It.*

Since 1967, Kenneth has been a minister of the gospel of Christ and teacher of God's Word. He is also the artist on award-winning albums such as his Grammy-nominated *Only the Redeemed, In His Presence, He Is Jehovah, Just a Closer Walk* and *Big Band Gospel.* He also co-stars as the character Wichita Slim in the children's adventure videos *The Gunslinger, Covenant Rider* and the movie *The Treasure of Eagle Mountain,* and as Daniel Lyon in the Commander Kellie and the Superkids™ videos *Armor of Light* and *Judgment: The Trial of Commander Kellie.* Kenneth also co-stars as a Hispanic godfather in the 2009 and 2016 movies *The Rally* and *The Rally 2: Breaking the Curse.*

With the help of offices and staff in the United States, Canada, England, Australia, South Africa and Ukraine, Kenneth is fulfilling his vision to boldly preach the uncompromised WORD of God from the top of this world, to the bottom, and all the way around. His ministry reaches millions of people worldwide through daily and Sunday TV broadcasts, magazines, teaching audios and videos, conventions and campaigns, and the World Wide Web.

Learn more about Kenneth Copeland Ministries by visiting our website at **kcm.org**

When The LORD first spoke to Kenneth and Gloria Copeland
about starting the *Believer's Voice of Victory* magazine...

He said: *This is your seed. Give it to everyone who ever responds to your ministry, and don't ever allow anyone to pay for a subscription!*

For more than 50 years, it has been the joy of Kenneth Copeland Ministries to bring the good news to believers. Readers enjoy teaching from ministers who write from lives of living contact with God, and testimonies from believers experiencing victory through God's WORD in their everyday lives.

Today, the *BVOV* magazine is mailed monthly, bringing encouragement and blessing to believers around the world. Many even use it as a ministry tool, passing it on to others who desire to know Jesus and grow in their faith!

Request your FREE subscription to the
Believer's Voice of Victory magazine today!

Go to **freevictory.com** to subscribe online, or call us at
1-800-600-7395 (U.S. only) or **+1-817-852-6000**.

We're Here for You!®

Your growth in God's WORD and victory in Jesus are at the very center of our hearts. In every way God has equipped us, we will help you deal with the issues facing you, so you can be the **victorious overcomer** He has planned for you to be.

The mission of Kenneth Copeland Ministries is about all of us growing and going together. Our prayer is that you will take full advantage of all The LORD has given us to share with you.

Wherever you are in the world, you can watch the *Believer's Voice of Victory* broadcast on television (check your local listings), the Internet at kcm.org or on our digital Roku channel.

Our website, **kcm.org,** gives you access to every resource we've developed for your victory. And, you can find contact information for our international offices in Africa, Australia, Canada, Europe, Ukraine and our headquarters in the United States.

Each office is staffed with devoted men and women, ready to serve and pray with you. You can contact the worldwide office nearest you for assistance, and you can call us for prayer at our U.S. number, 1-817-852-6000, seven days a week!

We encourage you to connect with us often and let us be part of your everyday walk of faith!

Jesus Is LORD!

Kenneth & Gloria Copeland

Kenneth and Gloria Copeland